COUNTY FAIR

by Ellen Garin illustrated by Elizabeth Wolf

Harcourt

Orlando   Boston   Dallas   Chicago   San Diego

Visit *The Learning Site!*

www.harcourtschool.com

Summer is a great time of year! The corn is high. The apples are ripening. Baby animals have grown.

There are many things to do during the summer. You can go camping, swimming, or biking. You can play outside. The weather is warm and the days are longer in summer, too. You may live near a place where a county fair happens every summer.

A county fair is a mixture of a farm and a carnival. There are many different kinds of food to eat and many interesting animals to see. Let's visit a county fair.

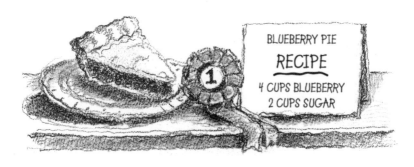

BLUEBERRY PIE
RECIPE
4 CUPS BLUEBERRY
2 CUPS SUGAR

The first thing you see at a county fair are the tents. Inside these tents are contests for skills, foods, and crafts.

The food tent displays prize-winning pies. At this fair, the blueberry pie has taken first prize! The prize-winning recipe calls for 4 cups of blueberries and 2 cups of sugar.

There are pint jars of jams and jellies. Some people like to eat jams or jellies on bread or toast. A pint is 16 ounces or two cups. Some people buy quart jars or 32 ounces of strawberry jam.

A farmer is selling cups of ice-cold lemonade. It is made from lemon juice, sugar, and water. It's hot under the tents and the people at the fair can be very thirsty. They line up to buy the lemonade. It tastes so good.

The farmer sells big gallon jugs of lemonade. A gallon is 128 ounces. A gallon is also 4 quarts, 8 pints, or 16 cups. A gallon is very heavy to carry!

3

County fairs started as events for farmers. At county fairs, farmers learn about better ways to grow things. Farmers also can buy and sell farm animals.

Farmers show their biggest and best pigs, cows, goats, and horses. Farmers and their families work hard all year to raise healthy animals. The healthiest and strongest animals win prizes. Blue ribbons are first prize. Red ribbons are second prize. Yellow ribbons are third prize.

Sometimes the winners receive a cash prize, too. Even children win prizes for animals they have raised. This girl's lamb has won a prize.

People also bring fruits and vegetables to show at county fairs. At county fairs, farmers discuss how to grow better fruits and vegetables.

Sometimes strange-looking fruits and vegetables are shown. Maybe they have a strange shape or they are very large. Sometimes there are prizes for the oddest looking fruits and vegetables.

5

It's fun to see the display of the largest fruits and vegetables.

Did you know that a pumpkin can weigh 800 pounds? The most exciting prize is given for the largest fruit or vegetable. How big can fruit and vegetables get?

- A watermelon can weigh 260 pounds. Some watermelons measure 3 1/2 feet around. Three and a half feet is 42 inches. Imagine how you would carry a watermelon that size home!

- Some tomatoes have weighed more than 20 pounds. Most of the time, tomatoes you see in stores weigh less than a pound.

County fairs can be competitive. There are often arm wrestling and walking races. Another favorite competition is the seed-spitting contest. People line up and spit watermelon seeds.

The person who spits the seeds farthest is the winner. This is the one time it's okay to spit for fun! Some people can spit a watermelon seed as far as 30 feet, or 10 yards!

You have to spit pretty hard to send a seed that far! It takes a lot of practice and a lot of watermelon!

Seed Spitting

Another contest is the watermelon-eating contest. A 40-pound watermelon is cut into four pieces. This means that each piece weighs 10 pounds.

Each person in the contest tries to eat all 10 pounds in one minute! That's a lot of watermelon to eat in 60 seconds!

Will the winner ever want to eat watermelon again?

Sometimes county fairs have tractor pull contests. Children and adults can take part in these contests.

Tractors are very important on farms. Tractors are used to plow fields and to gather crops. Tractors are used to drag heavy machines and animals from one side of the farm to the other. Farmers are proud of their tractors. The more weight a tractor can pull, the better.

In a tractor pull contest, people want to see how far a tractor can pull a heavy weight. If a tractor is pulling something that is too heavy, the tractor stops. The tractor cannot move another inch.

The judges measure how far each tractor has gone. Even kids can enter a tractor pull contest. Kids' tractors pull from 800 pounds to 1,500 pounds.

Adults' tractors pull more weight. Their tractors can pull from 6,500 to 30,000 pounds. A tractor that can pull 30,000 pounds is very big!

Many county fairs have rodeos. The people in the rodeos ride horses and bulls. They do tricks with ropes.

Everyone likes to watch the rodeo. First there is a parade. Cowboys and cowgirls ride their horses around the rodeo ring. The horses are beautiful!

There are seats around the rodeo ring. The seats are filled with cheering people. The people watch the cowboys test their skills.

Cowboys try to win money and ribbons in the rodeo contests. Some cowboys ride wild horses. These horses don't like to carry people, so they try to make the cowboys fall off.

Some cowboys ride bucking bulls. The bulls try to throw the cowboys off. It is hard to stay on a rodeo horse or bull. Riding a bucking horse or a bucking bull is a test of a cowboy's skill.

Other contests in the rodeo are timed contests. Rodeo contests are timed in seconds. One timed contest is barrel riding. Boys and girls can enter the barrel riding contests.

In a barrel riding contest, riders have to guide their horses around three barrels. Riders use their legs to guide the horses. The rider hangs on tight to the horse. The rider with the fastest time wins. Barrel riding lets the rider show how well he or she can ride.

Usually a county fair will have a midway. The midway is the carnival or amusement part of the fair. This is where the rides and games are. Some people think the midway is the best part of the fair.

Many county fairs have a roller coaster. Some roller coasters go 50 miles per hour. That's almost as fast as cars travel on a highway!

Usually roller coaster cars climb up a big hill. Then they drop down the other side. Many people scream and cheer on the way down.

Some county fairs have a carousel. A carousel is also called a merry-go-round. The carousel has horses and chariots to ride.

People who don't want to ride a horse sit in a chariot. Usually four people can sit in each chariot. The wooden horses are painted in bright colors, and the top of the carousel is decorated with beautiful flashing lights.

When the music starts, the carousel starts. The horses go up and down. The carousel goes around and around. Everyone loves the carousel. Some people try to grab the brass ring to get a free ride!

Sometimes there is a fun house at the county fair. People like to look at themselves in the fun-house mirrors. These mirrors make everyone look strange.

Some people like to play the games of skill on the midway. Some people throw darts at balloons. If they hit a balloon they win a prize.

Other people try to win a goldfish at the coin toss. If they can get a quarter in the bowl, they win a goldfish.

A county fair may have a Ferris wheel. A Ferris wheel is a large wheel that has seats people can sit in. Usually it's the tallest ride at the fair. Everyone lines up to get their turn.

The cars go around on the Ferris wheel. Two or three people sit in one car. Sometimes the people riding on the Ferris wheel can see the whole fair from the top of the ride.

Going to a county fair is a fun way to spend a summer day. There are so many things to do and to see!